Frederick Douglass

by Dana Meachen Rau

Compass Point Early Biographies

Content Adviser: Stephanie Davenport, Ed.D.,
DuSable Museum of African-American History, Chicago, Illinois

Reading Adviser: Dr. Linda D. Labbo,
Department of Reading Education, College of Education,
The University of Georgia

COMPASS POINT BOOKS

Minneapolis, Minnesota

Compass Point Books
3109 West 50th Street, #115
Minneapolis, MN 55410

Visit Compass Point Books on the Internet at *www.compasspointbooks.com*
or e-mail your request to *custserv@compasspointbooks.com*

Photographs ©: Corbis, cover, cover background, 22; North Wind Picture Archives, 4, 5 (bottom), 11, 15, 18, 21; Stock Montage, 5 (top), 10, 17, 24; Hulton-Deutsch Collection/Corbis, 6; Hulton/Archive by Getty Images, 8, 16, 23, 26; Réunion des Musées Nationaux/Art Resource, N.Y., 9; Library of Congress, 12, 20, 25; Scala/Art Resource, N.Y., 14; Joseph Sohm/ChromoSohm Inc./Corbis, 27.

Editors: E. Russell Primm, Emily J. Dolbear, and Catherine Neitge
Photo Researcher: Svetlana Zhurkina
Photo Selector: Linda S. Koutris
Designer/Page Production: Bradfordesign, Inc./Erin Scott, SARIN creative

Library of Congress Cataloging-in-Publication Data
Rau, Dana Meachen, 1971–
　Frederick Douglass / by Dana Rau.
　　　p. cm.— (Compass Point early biographies)
Includes bibliographical references and index.
Contents: Slaves in the South—Plantation life—A love of learning—Escape to freedom—Speaking out against slavery—Douglass the writer—The Civil War—A great leader—Important dates in Douglass's life.
　ISBN 0-7565-0418-X (hardcover)
　1. Douglass, Frederick, 1817?–1895—Juvenile literature. 2. African American abolitionists—Biography—Juvenile literature. 3. Abolitionists—United States—Biography—Juvenile literature. 4. Antislavery movements—United States—History—19th century—Juvenile literature. [1. Douglass, Frederick, 1817?–1895. 2. Abolitionists. 3. African Americans—Biography.] I. Title. II. Series.
　E449.D75 R39 2003
　973.8'092—dc21　　　　　　　　　　　　　　　2002009919

Table of Contents

*Note: In this book, words that are defined in the glossary are in **bold** the first time they appear in the text.*

Slaves in the South

America is home to many types of people. Today, all Americans are free.

For a long time in the past, however, people in the United States were not treated equally. Black people were taken by force from their homes in Africa. Many were sent to countries such as Cuba and Brazil. Some were sold as slaves to white men from the

Many slaves worked on large farms, such as this cotton plantation.

Southern American states who owned large farms, called **plantations.**

A grand plantation home in Mississippi

Most slave owners were white people. Some lived in grand houses, ate large meals, and wore fancy clothes. The slaves who worked for them, however, were sometimes treated poorly. One of these slaves was Frederick Augustus Washington Bailey.

◄ Africans were taken from their homes and sold as slaves.

Plantation Life

Frederick Bailey was born sometime in 1818 on a plantation in Talbot County, Maryland. He did not know his exact birthday. He believed he was born sometime in February. Slave owners did not record the birth of children who were born slaves.

Frederick did not know his mother, Harriet Bailey, well. She worked on a different plantation and died when Frederick was only seven. Frederick did not even know who his father was. His grandparents, Betsy and Isaac Bailey, cared for him until he was six and old enough to work. Then he was taken away

◀ Slave children were often separated from their parents at an early age.

For dinner, some slaves might have eaten mush from troughs like those used to feed pigs.

from his grandparents and moved to the plantation owned by Aaron Anthony.

Here Frederick saw how horrible slavery could be. Many slave owners beat and whipped their slaves. Even children were treated badly. Some were fed corn mush out of a **trough**. Troughs were usually used to feed animals. Most slaves were given only two shirts a year. They had no shoes, socks, or pants. Some slaves slept on the clay floor of their cabins without blankets. Frederick's bed was an empty corn sack.

Frederick Douglass arrived in Baltimore, Maryland, in 1826.

A Love of Learning

Frederick was glad to leave the plantation in 1826. He was sent to the city of Baltimore, Maryland. There he worked for Hugh and Sophia Auld, relatives of his owner. Life as a city slave was much different from life on the

Sophia Auld taught young
Frederick how to read.

plantation. Frederick ate good meals and slept in a comfortable bed.

Sophia was kind to Frederick. She taught him how to read. When her husband found out, he was furious. He did not believe slaves should know how to read.

Frederick loved learning. He gave poor white boys in the neighborhood extra bread so they would teach him to write. Instead of pens and paper, he used chalk to write on fences, walls, and sidewalks.

Frederick was eventually sent back to the plantation, where his master was cruel to him.

In 1833, Frederick was sent back to work on the plantation. He tried to teach other slaves how to read and write. His owner treated him horribly. Frederick planned to escape, but he was discovered. He was sent back to Baltimore in 1836.

Escape to Freedom

This time in Baltimore, Frederick worked in the **shipyards**. At that time, he met a free black woman named Anna Murray. He liked her very much.

City life was better than plantation life, but Frederick was unhappy. He did not like being owned by someone else.

Some black people traveled to the Northern states to escape slavery. It was against the law there. If the runaway slaves were caught, they were returned to their owners and punished. In 1838, Frederick planned another escape. He dressed up as a

◄ Anna Murray Douglass

Douglass escaped by dressing as a sailor and boarding a train to New York.

sailor and took a train to New York. Luckily no one stopped him or asked him questions. He had escaped!

Frederick was scared. He had no job, and he had no place to stay. He met David Ruggles, a black man who helped runaway slaves. He told

Frederick that he would be safer in
Massachusetts. So Frederick sent for Anna. They married and moved together to New Bedford, Massachusetts. Ruggles and other free blacks

Frederick and Anna found it safe to live in the coastal town of New Bedford, Massachusetts.

helped them move and find housing. Frederick changed his last name to Douglass. He knew that using his real name would make it easier for his owner to find him.

Speaking Out Against Slavery

Douglass enjoyed his life in New Bedford. He and Anna started a family. Over time, they had five children. Frederick became interested in the work of **abolitionists**. They were people who believed slavery was wrong. Douglass started to go to abolitionist meetings. At these meetings, black and white people met to talk about ways to get equal rights for all.

At a meeting in 1841,

An abolitionist poster speaking out against laws that punished runaway slaves

Douglass was asked to tell the people about his life. He was a great speaker. He was tall, and he had a strong voice. Soon, Douglass was giving speeches all over New England, New York, and the Ohio Valley. He met other famous abolitionists such as William Garrison, Sojourner Truth, and Susan B. Anthony.

Frederick Douglass was a powerful writer and speaker.

Douglass the Writer

In 1845, Douglass decided to write a book about his life as a slave. The book was called *Narrative of the Life of Frederick Douglass*. He was afraid he would be sent back into slavery when the book came out, however. So he went to Great Britain. He liked living there. Black people were treated the same as white people.

Douglass missed America and his family. If he went back to America, though, he would be caught. Some of his new friends in England decided to buy Douglass's freedom. They paid his owner $711.66. Finally, Douglass was free.

◀ Douglass traveled to Great Britain and gave speeches about the horrors of slavery.

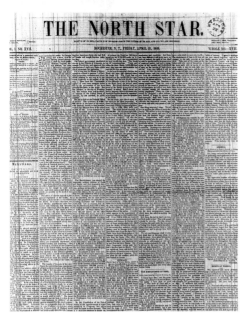

Douglass's newspaper, *The North Star*

Douglass returned to America in 1847. Many slaves were escaping to the North. Douglass thought it was important for them to have information. So he started his own newspaper. He called it *The North Star*, after the star that many slaves followed when they escaped. The paper became famous for speaking out against slavery and the unfair treatment of other groups, such as women. It was read by people as far away as Europe and the West Indies.

The Battle of Gettysburg was one of many bloody fights ▶ between the North and South during the Civil War.

The Civil War

From 1861 to 1865 the Northern and Southern states fought against each other in the American Civil War. The North didn't want slavery to spread to the other states. The South wanted to keep slavery. Douglass thought it was important for black people to

This drummer boy was one of many African-Americans who served in the Northern army.

be able to fight for the North during the Civil War. At first, black people were not allowed to join the army. Then, in 1862, President Abraham Lincoln allowed freed blacks to enlist in the Northern army.

In 1863, President Abraham Lincoln formally issued the **Emancipation Proclamation**. It stated that black slaves in Southern states were free. It

Two years after Lincoln's Emancipation Proclamation, Congress celebrated the passage of the 13th Amendment, which officially ended slavery. ➤

also said that freed black people from the South could join the Northern army. Finally, slavery was coming to an end. Many runaway slaves had enlisted in the Northern army after the Civil War broke out. The Emancipation Proclamation also said that these slaves could not be forced to return to their owners. Douglass met with President Lincoln soon

NARRATIVE

OF THE

LIFE

OF

FREDERICK DOUGLASS,

AN

AMERICAN SLAVE.

WRITTEN BY HIMSELF.

BOSTON:
PUBLISHED AT THE ANTI-SLAVERY OFFICE,
No. 25 Cornhill.
1846.

This book is the first of many Douglass wrote.

after that procla-mation. He want-ed to be sure all black soldiers were treated fair-ly and given the same pay as white soldiers.

Douglass greeting African-Americans in his government office ➤

A Great Leader

After the Civil War ended, Douglass contin-
ued to give speeches. He wrote more books.
He was a leader for the free black people in
the South.

In 1872, Douglass moved to Washington,
D.C., to work for the government. He also
worked to get **Congress** to pass a law giving
black people the right to vote.

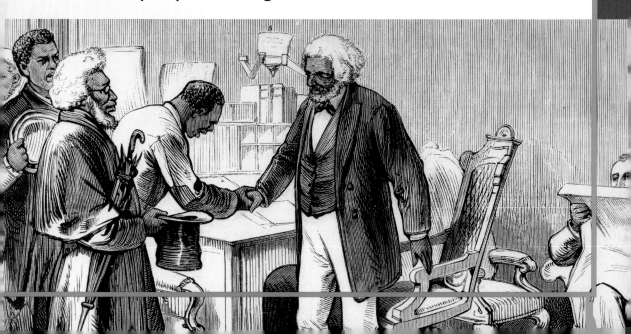

Douglass believed that everyone in America should be treated fairly. He thought every American should have the chance to learn to read and write. Above all, he believed that everyone should have freedom.

The grave of Frederick Douglass in Rochester, New York

Douglass died in 1895. He was seventy-seven years old. America lost a great leader, but his ideas helped make America a better nation for all people.

◄ Frederick Douglass went from being a slave to becoming an important leader for African-Americans.

Important Dates in Frederick Douglass's Life

1818	Born in Maryland
1824	Starts to work on Aaron Anthony's plantation
1826	Works in Baltimore for Hugh and Sophia Auld
1833	Sent to work on the plantation of Thomas Auld
1836	Goes back to Baltimore
1838	Escapes to New York; marries Anna Murray on September 15 and moves to New Bedford, Massachusetts
1841	Gives first speech at abolitionist meeting
1845	Writes *Narrative of the Life of Frederick Douglass*; goes to Great Britain
1846	Friends in England purchase his freedom
1847	Returns to America a free man; starts *The North Star* newspaper
1861–1865	The American Civil War is fought between the North and the South
1863	Emancipation Proclamation is issued by President Abraham Lincoln; Douglass meets Lincoln
1872	Moves to Washington, D.C.
1895	Dies on February 20

Glossary

abolitionists—people who spoke out against slavery

Congress—part of the U.S. government that makes the laws

Emancipation Proclamation—a document signed on January 1, 1863, by President Abraham Lincoln that freed slaves in the South

plantations—large farms where crops such as cotton were grown

shipyards—places where ships are built

trough—a long, low container used for feeding animals

Did You Know?

- Frederick Douglass did not know his birthday. He celebrated his birthday on February 14, Valentine's Day, because his mother used to call him "little valentine."

- When Douglass was thirteen, he saved up 50 cents by shining shoes to buy his first book, *The Columbian Orator*. It was filled with speeches by famous people.

- Almost two hundred thousand African-American soldiers fought for the North in the Civil War.

Want to Know More?

At the Library

Miller, William. *Frederick Douglass: The Last Day of Slavery*. New York: Lee and Low Books, 1995.

Schaefer, Lola M. *Frederick Douglass*. Mankato, Minn.: Pebble Books, 2002.

On the Web

American Visionaries: Frederick Douglass
http://www.cr.nps.gov/museum/exhibits/douglass/
To learn more about Frederick Douglass's life and times

African-American World
http://www.pbs.org/wnet/aaworld/
For a biography of Frederick Douglass and other African-Americans

Through the Mail

The Frederick Douglass Museum and Cultural Center
25 East Main Street, Suite 500
Rochester, NY 14614
716/546-3960
For information on Frederick Douglass and his influence on the world

On the Road

Frederick Douglass National Historic Site
1411 W Street, S.E.
Washington, DC 20020
202/426-5961
To see Douglass's home and learn more about his life

31

Index

About the Author
Dana Meachen Rau is a children's book author, editor, and illustrator. She has written more than seventy-five books, including nonfiction, biographies, early readers, and historical fiction. She is a graduate of Trinity College in Hartford, Connecticut. Dana works from her home office in Burlington, Connecticut, where she lives with her husband, Chris, and children, Charlie and Allison.